Auras

Learn How to Read and Cleanse Auras

By Sarah Martin & Barbara Rowland

Contents

Introduction

The practice of reading auras is something that has gained popularity in recent years. One reason for this is an increased interest in spiritual matters. Many believe that the ability to see a person's aura is nothing less than the ability to see that person's soul. Another reason, however, has to do with scientific discoveries regarding the bio-energy field of all living things. According to modern science, an aura is nothing more than the electrical signature of a living being. In either case, the information that an aura can reveal regarding an individual is remarkable. By reading a person's aura you can determine their personality, state of mind and even physical health. Whether you choose to regard auras as proof of the immortal soul, or you choose to see them as simple energy signatures, the fact remains that you can develop an ability to see and read them.

This book will reveal techniques explaining how to read auras, as well as information to help you interpret the information auras reveal. Additionally, several chapters of this book are dedicated to the basic aspects of auras including proof of their existence, where they can be found, who can read them and the moral and ethical implications of aura reading. By the time you finish reading this book, you will know the truth about auras and the function they serve. Furthermore, you will be able to develop the ability to both see and interpret auras, thereby enabling you to gain a deeper understanding of the people around you, your personal life and even life itself. Welcome to the fascinating world of reading auras!

Part 1: The Nature of Auras

Chapter 1: Are Auras Real?

Before you begin studying the various techniques on how to read auras, the first question you have to answer is whether or not auras are even real. You are probably reading this book because you have heard about auras but have never actually seen one. Whether you have merely read about them or you know someone who can see them, the simple fact is that until you see one for yourself, you have to take the word of others regarding whether or not auras actually exist. For many people, the old axiom "seeing is believing" holds true in the case of auras. Unfortunately, since you have to believe that they exist before you can put any effort into being able to see them for yourself, this axiom can undermine any real chances of success.

This chapter will cover the various forms of evidence that support the reality of auras. The information presented will help you to decide whether you believe that auras are real or just a hoax used by would-be clairvoyants, fortune tellers and the like. However, with the overwhelming evidence supporting the existence of auras, it is likely that you will leave this chapter a full-fledged believer.

The scientific argument against auras

Before exploring the arguments supporting the reality of auras it is important to first explore the arguments that try to disprove their existence. Only when you are able to weigh the merits of both sides can you come to a solid and convincing conclusion of your own. That said, there are several scientific arguments that state auras are not as they seem. Instead, they are easily explained away as a phenomenon that can trick people into thinking they see something that isn't there, or that they simply misinterpret what they are actually seeing. Interestingly enough, none of these arguments deny that people are able to see *something*. Instead, they simply try to explain what is seen as something far less significant than auras.

One argument against the existence of auras is that of synesthesia. This is a neurological phenomenon experienced by a very low percentage of people around the world. In short, synesthesia is when the physical senses become mingled, creating different mental experiences than what you would expect from specific sensory input. In such a case a person who smells a pie baking in the oven might see colors in their mind that their brain associates with the smell. Alternatively, a person might experience a sense of smell when seeing a specific color. This is where the mind interprets one type of sensory input in unique and unexpected ways. How this is related to auras is really quite simple. The idea is that a person can see colors around someone based on how they feel about that person. This is the mind taking intuitive input and creating a visual

3

response from it. Therefore, the theory of synesthesia states that the aura is a construct within the mind, interpreting intuitive and other input in a visual way. In other words, it's all in the mind.

Another argument against auras is that they are the result of microorganisms, dust, fungus and a whole host of other "nastiness" that exists on the human body. This theory suggests that dead skin cells, microbes, and the like form a sort of halo around the body referred to as the microbiome. Every person has a unique microbiome, determined by their chemistry, hygiene, health and other such factors. This explains why every person seems to have a unique aura around their body. Like an aura, the microbiome extends around your whole body, creating a cloud of living and dead material, all organic in nature, that can be picked up on certain photographic equipment, or even by the naked eye under certain specific conditions. In short, this explanation suggests that the aura is nothing more or less than an envelope of skin cells, microbes and other microscopic particles that are ordinarily invisible to the naked eye.

The scientific argument for auras

Despite the fact that there are a significant number of scientists who reject the existence of auras there are many who actually do believe in them. While these scientists may not regard auras as proof of the immortal soul, or that they are capable of revealing a person's true nature, they nevertheless believe that auras are real. These scientists provide several theories to explain what auras are and how they should be interpreted. Again, even though these arguments might try to explain away the significance of auras, they do not try to deny their existence. Therefore, all arguments so far accept some level of reality with regard to the aura phenomenon.

One theory to explain the existence of auras is the energy theory. Science has long known that the human body produces electromagnetic signals, sending information from all parts of the body to the brain and back again. These signals are how we feel everything from pain to pleasure and everything in between. Modern technological advances have made it possible to not only measure such electromagnetic signatures but to also see them. This ability has its value in the field of medicine where electrocardiograms and other tests measure the energy field created by various organs within the body. Based on this understanding of the electromagnetic nature of the human body scientists have concluded that there is a virtual envelope of energy surrounding every person's body. This is their explanation of what auras are.

The field of physics has added to the theory of auras being energy with its latest understanding regarding the true nature of physical matter. For countless years humanity has separated tangible things into the categories of liquid, solid and gas. However, recent studies suggest that solid objects may not be solid at all. Instead, it is now believed that everything is actually energy, just vibrating on different frequencies. In other words, a piece of wood is nothing more or less than a field of energy vibrating at a very low frequency, making it seem solid as a result. The slower the vibration, the more solid or dense an object becomes. By contrast, rapidly vibrating energy will appear as electricity, light and other non-solid phenomena. Thus, the question physicists are asking isn't whether or not auras are real, but whether or not *matter* is real! Based on this theory, all living matter is energy. Therefore the ability to see auras around a person or object is nothing exceptional at all.

Auras in religion

While science can be a good place to go for rational arguments and logical opinions it should never be the only place you go to for proof as to whether something exists or not. Another good place to go for such answers is religion. This isn't to suggest that you need to subscribe to what a particular religion teaches or believes, instead it is to say that if multiple religions agree on a matter, then there might be some validity to the matter itself. Auras, like the afterlife, divine beings, and other such spiritual topics, can be found in multiple religious traditions. Therefore, it is worth seeing what these traditions have to say about the existence of auras and what they actually mean.

One of the oldest religions known to man is the Hindu religion. Originating in India, Hinduism is a rich and vibrant tradition, providing explanations to every possible experience in life, death and everything in between. Strangely enough, the energy field around the human body that science has 'recently discovered' is described in ancient Hindu texts predating the very founding of Christianity! These texts suggest that every physical body has a subtle body, which is a body of energy that reflects the physical form. This subtle body is made up of energy that emanates from several key points along an axis. These points are commonly referred to as chakras, a term many people are familiar with. Each chakra is responsible for a specific type of energy, and the health of the chakra equates to the health of the energy it produces. In the end, not only does the Hindu tradition subscribe to auras but it also explains how auras are formed, their role in life and how they can be 'fixed' should they be injured or misaligned.

While it might not be surprising that a mystical tradition such as Hinduism teaches about the human aura what might surprise many people is that Judaism and Christianity make reference to auras as well. It is reported in the Old Testament that when Moses came down from the mountain where he talked to God the "glory of God shown around him". While this can be argued as not referring to the aura there is no doubt that a certain glow emanated from Moses after his divine encounters. It is entirely possible that this glow was the aura of Moses, simply made more evident after his interactions with God. Since the average person at the time had no way of knowing what an aura was, they could have explained it as the "glory of God" for lack of any better description. In any case, the glow described fits the description of an aura perfectly.

Christianity also makes reference to the "glory of God" in the New Testament. Events, where the disciples are filled with the Holy Spirit, result in the disciples being "bathed in the glory of God", another attempt at explaining an otherworldly glow that surrounded the body of an individual. Again, whether you believe that this refers to the aura or the "glory of God," it nevertheless fits the description of an aura perfectly.

The bottom line

In the end, it is up to you to decide what you believe. The bottom line, however, is that no argument made for or against actually attempts to debunk the phenomenon of an aura altogether. At worst, arguments against simply try to explain auras as something less significant and perfectly ordinary. Alternatively, the number of traditions that describe auras as real and significant should give you plenty of food for thought when it comes to deciding what you believe. Even if you don't believe in a particular religion, to see that several religions describe the same phenomenon should be enough to suggest that the phenomenon is real. And, since both science and religion seem to agree to that point, it seems safe enough to say that auras are, in fact, very real.

Chapter 2: Does Everyone Possess an Aura?

One question that pops up from time to time is whether or not everyone possesses an aura. This is usually due to how a person perceives auras. Some traditions treat auras as a sign of spiritual advancement, so it would stand to reason that not everyone would have one as few people could be considered spiritually advanced. While it would be safe to assume that such people as the Dali Lama, the Pope, and other religious leaders may have reached the level of spiritual advancement needed to acquire an aura you wouldn't assume the same of the average person walking the street. However, other traditions treat auras as a part of life that all living things share. In this light not only do all people possess an aura, but every single living thing possesses an aura, regardless of spiritual advancement, intellectual capability or the like. In the end, there are far more traditions, both religious and scientific, that believes everyone possesses an aura than there are traditions that don't. This chapter will explore the various reasons why.

The scientific explanation

The overall consensus within the scientific circles that subscribe to the existence of auras is that all people possess one. This is because the nature of auras is distinctly different in the minds of scientists than it is in the minds of the religious. Rather than being seen as a spiritual attainment, auras are understood to be energy fields, nothing more and nothing less. And, since all living things possess energy all living things must also possess auras. Subsequently, the only reason something wouldn't possess an aura is if that particular thing weren't actually alive. However, as long as something, or someone, is alive, they must have energy flowing through them, and this energy is what creates the aura that you can learn to see and read.

This belief that all living things possess energy, and thus an energy field, opens up a whole new level for who and what possess auras. Not only do all people possess auras in this tradition, but all animals, plants, fish, and birds as well. In short, every single living thing, from people to microscopic wiggly things, possesses an energy field of some form. While these fields are stronger and more pronounced in larger more animated life forms such as people, they are nevertheless just as present and observable in such things as plants and trees. Studies have been done to measure the energy flowing through plants, and whether that energy changes based on certain stimuli. The results have conclusively shown that even plants have energy-based responses to external factors, just as you would expect in a person. Therefore, the energy field commonly associated with people is actually something that serves to connect every living thing in our world.

As if that weren't mind-blowing enough, another scientific

theory takes the energy field to an even higher level. According to this theory, matter itself is nothing more or less than energy vibrating at a low level. Thus, the difference between light and matter is nothing more than the rate at which energy vibrates. Fast vibrating energy will create light, whereas slower vibrating energy will create people, and even slower vibrating energy will create rocks, sand and all things commonly referred to as "inanimate". Thus, not only do all living things have an aura, but even all non-living things do, seeing as all things in existence are merely a form or expression of energy. This means that absolutely everything possesses an aura. However, since inanimate objects vibrate on such a low frequency, it is possible that their energy would go unnoticed even to someone capable of seeing and reading auras.

The spiritual explanation

The spiritual explanation of auras creates a bit of a different narrative concerning who or what possesses one. As stated before, some religious traditions see auras as something acquired as the result of spiritual enlightenment. Such traditions not only dismiss the idea that all people possess an aura but they also wholly dismiss any notion that all living things have one. Needless to say, they would also reject the notion that rocks and other inanimate objects could have an aura of any form or frequency. That said, most religious traditions actually believe that all people do have an aura. This is because those traditions view the aura as the immortal soul. Therefore, regardless of how spiritually enlightened a person is, each and every person has to possess an aura.

Unfortunately, this is where the general consensus between different religious traditions begins to fall apart. Certain traditions, especially within Christianity, believe that only people possess souls. As a result, these traditions believe that only people would be able to possess an aura. Even though plants and animals are alive, they are not seen as having a soul; therefore they cannot possibly have an aura. The main reason behind this belief is the notion that man was created in the image of God. Thus, only man has an immortal soul that reflects the true nature of God himself.

Alternatively, other religions, especially those of a more mystical nature such as Buddhism, Hinduism, and even mystical traditions within Judaism and Christianity believe that all living things possess a soul of sorts. This reflects the idea that a soul is needed for a thing to actually be alive. Shamans in Africa and the Amazon have very specific rituals, which they perform when picking berries or other organic ingredients for a medicinal potion, which give thanks to the plant they are picking the ingredients from. The idea is that the plant will react more positively when you show gratitude than if you simply take what you want. This is one example of the belief that all living things possess a very real and intelligent soul. Since the aura is seen as the soul, this belief would suggest that all living things would necessarily possess one.

Overall consensus

Unfortunately, there is no single consensus regarding who or what can possess an aura. However, one thing that is interesting is the fact that both science and religion seem to have three distinct beliefs. The first belief is that only certain life has an aura, specifically people and larger animals. This fits into the scientific theory regarding how much energy flows through such living things. Likewise, this matches the religious notion that only people have a soul since only people are in God's image. The second theory is that all living things have an aura. According to certain scientific circles, this is due to the fact that energy creates life; therefore all living things must have an energy field, which creates an aura. More mystical religious traditions share this belief since they equate the soul with life the same way that science equates energy with life. Thus, anything that lives has a soul, which is the source of an aura. Finally, the belief that everything that exists has an aura can also be found in both science and religion. This is due to the shared belief that matter is simply energy/soul, and thus, everything in existence has to have energy/soul in order to exist. Therefore, everything in existence must also have an aura.

The most interesting thing in this comparison is that the most advanced scientific theories seem to reflect the most mystical religious beliefs. It's as though the more you open your mind, either to science or spirituality, the more you discover. No matter what belief or theory you choose to follow, the important thing to remember is that most point to the notion that all people have auras. Since you will probably be focusing on reading other people, and possibly yourself, this is the only thing that matters. You don't have to believe that rocks or birds have auras in order to develop the ability to see and read the auras of people. It is, however, some very interesting food for thought!

Chapter 3: Auras and Energy Fields

When you look at the scientific and religious arguments that support the existence of auras you will find that they agree on the main premise that auras are the manifestation of an energy field. The causes and nature of this energy field may differ between the two establishments, but the fact that energy is at the heart of what auras are is very significant. By understanding each side of the argument, you get a more complete picture of what auras actually are. Whether you choose to believe the scientific explanation, the spiritual explanation or a combination of the two is entirely up to you. The important thing is to realize that even though the explanations differ in certain ways, they both end up stating the same conclusion, namely that auras do indeed exist.

The scientific explanation

As mentioned earlier, the advent of modern technological advances has enabled us to see things that no one could ever have hoped to see in times past. One example of this is the electrical activity of different organs within the human body. Electrocardiograms, or EKGs for short, are tests that are performed to measure the electrical activity of a person's heartbeat. This means that the heart generates a specific electrical signature as it pumps the blood through your veins. The same thing happens with the brain as it processes information and sends signals to the rest of the body. This is measured by a test known as electroencephalography, or EEG for short. An EEG measures the electrical signature of the brain, determining how active the brain is and whether or not there are any anomalies. While this may not seem overly significant regarding auras it presents a very real argument for what auras actually are.

The important thing to realize at this point is that energy can be seen in different ways. One way is by measuring the heat that energy produces. No source of energy can exist without creating a heat signature that is greater than if the energy were not present. It's a bit like having an oven on as opposed to having it off. What makes the oven heat up is energy. When energy is present, the oven is hot. Alternatively, when energy is not present the oven is cold. Everything reacts to energy this way. Another way that energy reveals itself is through light. Again, if you imagine your oven heating up, not only do the coils get hot but they also glow as they heat up. Thus, the energy you release when you turn your oven on creates both heat and light. This is a very important thing to understand when it comes to auras.

Science agrees that all living things possess a bio-energy field that permeates and surrounds the body. Since energy creates both heat and light (at high levels), then it stands to reason that every living being would have a heat and light signature as a result of their particular bio-energy field. This would suggest that auras are this signature, the light and heat created by the energy that flows through each and every one of us.

The spiritual explanation

Interestingly enough, spiritual traditions that believe in auras also believe that each and every living being possesses an energy field of sorts. Different traditions will have different names for this field, such as spirit, soul, energy or any number of terms specific to the tradition or the language of its followers. Still, the important thing to focus on isn't the difference in terminology, rather the important thing is that each term refers to the same phenomenon—an energy field. That the spiritual explanation and the scientific explanation are in such agreement is a miracle unto itself, seeing as these two disciplines tend to disagree on the nature of just about everything else.

Furthermore, the fact that religion believes that energy is required for life is highly significant. Just as science has demonstrated that something can only be alive if it has a properly functioning bio-energy field, virtually all religions agree that something can only be alive if it possesses a soul. When the soul leaves the body, this is the point of death. Alternatively, when the soul enters the body, this is the point of true life. And, just as science can measure the energy levels within the body to determine the physical health and wellbeing of an individual, so too, certain religious traditions measure a person's aura to assess their spiritual health and wellbeing. The biggest difference is that while science uses machines, x-ray equipment, and various photographic devices, religious healers simply rely on their ability to see the aura with the naked eye.

Chakras and their role

Perhaps the most amazing thing about the spiritual tradition of auras is how exactly it matches the scientific understanding of the bio-energy field. Perhaps the most prominent example of this can be found in the tradition of chakras. It would take an entire book to cover the specifics of the seven chakras and their functions, however, for this book it is enough to simply present a basic understanding of them. The term "chakra" comes from the ancient Sanskrit word for "wheel". Originating in ancient Indian spiritual traditions, it is the belief that every person possesses seven chakras or wheels of energy within them. Each chakra serves a unique function, but all are tasked with receiving, producing or processing energy. When the chakras are properly aligned and functioning, the energy flows freely through the human body. However, when a chakra is misaligned, damaged or blocked the energy flow within the individual is adversely affected.

Another significant aspect of chakras is where they exist. If you look at a chakra map, you will see that the seven chakras line up along an axis that runs along the spinal column. Furthermore, each chakra seems to exist at or near a vital organ or physiological system, such as the heart, the head or the stomach and so on. Therefore, the chakra system can be seen as a spiritual equivalent to the biological systems in the body. Just as heart troubles will cause problems for the individual, so too, troubles in the heart chakra will cause similar problems. In a way, the chakra map is like an ancient spiritual depiction of the body and its different systems. That science has only now caught up to this ancient wisdom makes it that much more amazing!

How chakras relate to auras is fairly simple. Just as each

physiological system and organ in the human body creates an energy signature that manifests as the bio-field, so too, each chakra creates an energy signature that comprises the aura of the individual. Since auras can contain multiple layers and colors, the different chakras can have a very significant impact on the state of an aura as a whole. When one chakra is off, the aura will reflect not only a deficiency but the specific source of the deficiency. As you master the art of reading auras you will be able to notice these subtle signs and understand their true meaning.

What it all means

The fact that the bio-energy field of science and the aura/soul of religion are so similar in nature, purpose, and function there can be little room for doubt that this phenomenon actually exists. Again, it makes little difference as to whether you subscribe to the science of auras or their spiritual traditions. The important thing is that you come to realize two significant points. First, auras do in fact exist. The significance of science and religion agreeing on this point cannot be overstated. Second, auras can be seen, and therefore read. Whether you train yourself to see the bio-field or the human soul, the simple truth is that you will learn to see auras and understand the information they possess.

Part 2: Auras and Religion

Chapter 4: Is Aura Reading a Religious Practice?

While it's true that auras are currently as much a topic for scientific debate as they are for religious discussion the fact is that they were first embraced by religions that stretch back thousands of years. Different religions around the world have made reading auras a very real part of their practice, using the technique to determine the condition of a person's physical health, mental health and even spiritual health. In fact, there are as many names for an aura as there are religions on the planet. Each religion has recognized, embraced and even made use of auras in some way, shape or form. Therefore, the reading of auras can be seen not only as a religious practice but one that is as ancient as religion itself. Furthermore, the reading of auras can be seen as one of the few ways in which the spirit realm can be significantly experienced in the physical realm, thus creating a bridge that helps to expand our understanding of human existence.

Auras in India

The practice of reading auras can be found in all sorts of ancient tribal religions, including those in Africa, Australia, and South America. Unfortunately, most of these traditions lack any form of written history that would allow us to know just how ancient the practice actually is. Therefore, the oldest historical evidence regarding auras in religion belongs to India, where the Hindu tradition and its writings can be traced back into the very dawn of human history. Fortunately, not only do the Hindu texts help us to understand the ancient the practice of reading auras but they also help to demonstrate the significance of auras and the information they convey. A central belief in the Hindu tradition is that the aura of a person is their spirit or subtle body. Thus, being able to see a person's aura was nothing less than being able to see their very soul. This not only 'proved' the spirit world for early Hindu followers, but it also helped to show how the physical world was merely a reflection of the spirit world that existed just beneath it.

The significance of the aura carried over into another ancient and venerated Indian tradition—Buddhism. This makes perfect sense since the Buddha grew up in the midst of the Hindu tradition. Buddhists, like their Hindu forebears, believe that the aura is the subtle body of the individual. Certain colors have important meanings and reflect the spiritual development of the individual. The color of Gautama Buddha's aura is called Prabashvara in the Buddhist tradition. This color consists of five separate colors, combining to form a single hue. The five colors forming the Prabashvara are scarlet, blue, white, crimson, and yellow (golden yellow to be precise). These colors have very specific meanings in the Buddhist tradition, each signifying a unity to a particular aspect of life or existence. They can also be found in the chakra tradition, which is another aspect of the subtle body within each person.

The five colors of the Prabashvara were used to create a flag that has become universally accepted as the Buddhist flag. This incorporation of colors onto the flag is only one form of artistic expression regarding the aura. Other expressions can be found in such things as the lotus with its points of light as well as within mandala art, where mandalas represent either the universe as a whole or the inner soul of the individual. The constant incorporation of images and symbols related to the aura within the Hindu and Buddhist traditions serve to demonstrate just how significant auras and their readings are in those practices.

Auras in Chinese culture

Chinese culture is another in which auras have a very rich and ancient past. This can be explained in one of two ways. First, there is the idea that the ancient Chinese religions that pre-date Buddhism are nature religions, steeped in spiritualism much like African, Aboriginal and Amazonian religions. Thus, it has been theorized that the significance of auras in Chinese culture goes back to prehistory itself. The other theory is that the significance of the aura came into China with Buddhism. Regardless of which theory you accept the fact is that auras and the reading of auras play a very important role in Chinese religious and philosophical culture.

One of the ways the Chinese use auras in their religious practice is to identify illness. Traditions such as Reiki and Qigong rely on the healer's ability to see a person's aura in order to determine what techniques need to be applied to heal the patient. This reflects the Chinese belief that the energy of a person determines their overall health— physical, mental and spiritual. Known as "chi", this energy field is believed to exist in all matter, both living and inanimate. Any physical or mental illness can be traced to a block in the flow of the chi, and this is where the healer works their 'magic'. Some traditions use acupressure and acupuncture to restore the flow of chi energy, whereas others rely on massage techniques. Some traditions don't even require physical touch; instead they use the chi of the healer to connect with and invigorate the chi of the patient. In the end, the healing arts of Chinese religious practices have been around for thousands of years, bringing health and comfort to countless people during that time.

The chi energy also has certain applications within martial arts. While martial arts may not be seen as a religion by many the fact is that the arts were originally intended to be a mix of religious and non-religious teachings. In fact, martial arts were often used as a means to teach otherwise forbidden subjects in a subtle and covert way. The existence of chi energy is one such example. Not only do many martial art forms teach the existence of the chi, but they also develop a person's ability to use their chi in their martial arts exercises. The power behind a punch or kick in martial arts is more than mere physics; it is due to the extension of the chi energy. In essence, by extending their chi a martial arts fighter literally fights with their soul as well as their body.

Auras and spirituality worldwide

As mentioned earlier, auras can be found in just about every religion from every corner of the world and every era of human history. In fact, you would be hard pressed to find a true, established religion that didn't make some mention or reference to auras and the reading of auras. From tribal religions in the heart of Africa to the mystical traditions of Judaism and Christianity, auras can be found under many different names and with many different purposes. The one thing these religions do agree upon, however, is that auras are a very real representation of the spirit world and the immortal soul that each person possesses.

Interestingly enough, the reading of auras represents two distinct aspects of spirituality within the different religions. In some religions, the purpose of reading auras is to discern a person's health and wellbeing, especially in spiritual terms. This can be seen in the aforementioned Chinese traditions of Reiki and Qigong. However, there is another aspect of reading auras that focuses more on the reader than the subject. In this case, the ability to see and read auras is used as a measure of the spiritual progress a person is making. It is commonly believed that in order to see auras a person must open up their spiritual awareness. In some traditions, this is referred to as the opening of the third eye. Only when a person is in tune with their third eye or spiritual vision can they begin to see and read auras. Thus, in these traditions, the important thing is to nurture a person's innate spiritual abilities. The ability to read auras is the measure of this process.

In short, whether it's for determining a person's health and wellbeing, or it's for measuring an individual's spiritual abilities, reading auras is very much a religious practice in many cultures and traditions around the world. Within all these traditions the nature of the aura is seen as the soul of the individual, and thus it is seen as something very sacred. To be able to read a person's aura is equally sacred as this is the ability to virtually see the soul of another living being. Subsequently, the reading of auras is taken very seriously in all traditions, requiring devotion, practice and even guidance along the way.

Chapter 5: Do I have to be Religious to Read Auras?

The fact that the practice of reading auras is deeply rooted in many of the world's religions can be concerning to those who don't hold to any particular religious belief. After all, if reading auras require joining a certain church or tradition, it would require a person to change their whole worldview, and that could be seen as a price too steep to pay. Fortunately, even though reading auras is common in many religious circles, it doesn't mean that you have to be religious in order to do it. This is especially true in light of the fact that auras have become a subject of scientific interest in recent years. Considering the number of scientists who are atheist or agnostic you could hardly expect auras to be of serious scientific interest if religious faith were required. That said, there is a certain amount of faith needed in order to open your mind to the world of auras. Even though it's not faith in God as such, it is still faith nonetheless. At some point, you will have to believe in such things as energy, the role of energy in living matter and the interpretation of what you see. Furthermore, only when you believe that seeing auras is even possible should you go on to study the techniques for doing so.

Belief in energy

The first thing that you have to believe in when it comes to seeing and reading auras is energy itself. While most people have no trouble accepting the basic premise of energy, specifically related to electricity and such things as the combustion engine, some have a hard time accepting the idea that all matter is in fact, comprised of energy. This is where science and recent scientific discoveries can prove very useful. Physicists have theorized about the role of energy and matter for as long as physics has been around. In fact, one reason for this was to quantify the human soul. While most religions believed that the difference between a living person and a dead person was the presence of the soul, science had yet to come up with a similarly universal explanation. The idea that energy somehow played a role helped to achieve that goal.

Experiments on living, dying, and dead plants, animals and people led to some very interesting discoveries. Perhaps the greatest among these was the presence of energy. As modern technology advanced, the ability to measure electrical impulses, heat signatures and other aspects of energy within a living organism became easier and more accurate. This resulted in scientists being able to conclude that energy made all the difference between something being alive and something being dead. When something was alive it would give off heat, which could be measured using certain photographic devices. Alternatively, once something was dead this heat would diminish until it was gone altogether.

Likewise, electrical impulses could be detected in a living organism; however these would be absent once the organism was no longer alive. Therefore, the undeniable conclusion was that energy was the essence of life itself. Thus, all living things had energy flowing through them in some way, and this energy could be measured and even seen using the right equipment.

Again, believing in energy isn't as demanding as believing in a divine entity, the afterlife or some other concept that is less measurable. However, you still have to accept that there is an energy field that flows through and around your person, creating the very aura that you are hoping to see. Once you believe in the energy that creates auras you can allow yourself to study and practice the various ways in which to see and read them.

Faith in seeing beyond the normal spectrum

Believing in the energy that permeates all living things is only the beginning. Even if you accept that every person has an energy field in and around them that isn't to say that you believe in the ability to see such a field. This is especially true with regard to the naked eye. After all, while some types of photographic equipment, as well as other electronic devices, can measure and even perceive energy fields in and around living beings, this doesn't mean that you should be able to see those fields without the use of such devices. Unfortunately, this is where many people struggle the most. While they have no problem believing in energy, or even the human soul, they struggle with the belief that they can develop the ability to see such things with the naked eye. As a result, when results fail to come quickly or in the way expected, many people simply give up on ever being able to see and read auras.

This is where religion comes to the rescue. While you don't have to be religious in order to see or read auras the fact is that religion can provide you with the faith you need. That is because religions all across the world have known about auras for hundreds and thousands of years. Long before science created the necessary equipment to measure and photograph energy fields. Therefore, it has to be concluded that the ability to see auras with the naked eye existed far before the ability to detect and measure them with the use of technology.

Furthermore, the fact that different religions from different parts of the world and different eras of human history recognize the existence of auras means that people are able to see them and read them regardless of race, age, culture or even religious affiliation. If only one church or one religion believed in auras and practiced reading them, you could argue that it was either a local phenomenon or a hoax altogether. However, when numerous traditions that had no contact or common origin hold the same belief, you know that there is something important going on.

The most important thing to realize is that if so many cultures and traditions claim that auras can be seen then it must be true. It comes down to the old axiom "You can fool all of the people some of the time, and some of the people all of the time, but you can't fool all of the people all of the time". All of those traditions and religions couldn't have maintained a belief that wasn't true for so long without people getting wise to it. Therefore, it must be assumed that seeing auras is possible and even commonplace. It must also be assumed that if all these other people can do it then so can you!

Interpretation of what you see

After you reach the point where you believe in the energy of the auras and your ability to see them the next leap of faith comes with believing what you see. Seeing auras isn't a matter of turning a light switch on or off, so to speak. Instead, it is a progressive experience. In a way, it's a bit like learning to speak another language. You don't suddenly become fluent in another language overnight. Instead, you have to learn the rules, vocabulary and speech patterns of the language before becoming proficient in it. Soon you will be able to speak in that language, a bit broken at first, but understandable nonetheless. Eventually, you will become more and more fluent as you master the language through ongoing study and practice.

The same holds true for seeing and reading auras. While some may pick up on it quickly, others will have to put in more time and effort to get the results. Even so, there will be many results along the way. This is where belief is all important. At first, you might catch a glimpse of an aura or a color surrounding someone only to lose sight of it as quickly as you noticed it. All too often you might be tempted to explain the event away as a trick of sunlight, your eyes being tired or simply your imagination running wild. As tempting as this might be, it is vital to not fall into the trap of explaining any experience away. Instead, you should accept each and every experience as a progression along your journey to seeing and reading auras. This is a skill that has to be developed over time. Therefore, appreciate the fact that results may be few and fleeting at first. Only when you accept those results can you build on them. By believing in what you see you can train yourself to see more of the same. Alternatively, if you dismiss what you see, then you will keep yourself from ever making any real progress. Therefore, while you don't have to be religious in order to see auras you do need to have some good old-fashioned faith.

Chapter 6: Is It Anti-Christian to Read Auras?

There can be a great deal of concern when it comes to reading auras for anyone who regards themselves as a Christian. One of the main reasons for this is the number of warnings and taboos within the Bible regarding dabbling in spiritual matters. According to these passages to dabble with spiritualism is to play with fire. Even worse, it is to open the door to the king of fire himself—the devil. At the very least, experimenting in such practices can be seen as a sin, so no self-respecting Christian should want to risk doing the wrong thing even if it seems harmless enough. This chapter will address the concerns regarding the nature of auras and whether or not reading them is actually a sin. Both sides of the argument will be presented so that you can make a well-informed decision on how to proceed in your own life.

Arguments suggesting reading auras is a sin

The main argument raised against reading auras is that

doing so constitutes dabbling in spiritualism. This is a particularly significant issue in the Old Testament, where God's Chosen were constantly exposed to traditions and religions that summoned spirits, foretold the future and did such things as casting spells, curses and the like. Laws were written down forbidding such practices, calling them evil, satanic and most of all, very dangerous. It was believed that to do anything involving spirits was to court demons, devils and all sorts of dangerous and sinister beings. Not only could such practices harm a person in this life, but they could also harm a person's soul, meaning that they would suffer in the life beyond. Therefore, to the mind of the Israelite of the Old Testament, reading auras would be seen as dangerous and sinful.

This argument persists even into modern times. One of the main reasons for this is the association of reading auras with such groups as pagans, fortune tellers, spiritualists and a vast number of new age traditions. While auras and the reading of auras aren't unique to these groups, the association with them is enough for auras to get a bad reputation within Christian circles. Additionally, anyone who reads auras is seen as someone who may be interested in other spiritual practices. In a sense, reading auras is often seen as a gateway drug of sorts. While not necessarily bad unto itself, it is a practice, which can lead to other more sinister and dangerous practices down the road. Furthermore, the type of people you might associate with while reading auras may be the type to lead you away from the Christian path, thereby leading your soul to eternal damnation.

Another reason that many believe reading auras is sinful and dangerous is the idea that a person needs the help of another entity in order to see auras. According to this belief, a person can only read auras when they solicit the help of a spirit. This is why the average person can't see auras. Only by working with a spirit or demon can a person have their eyes opened to the spirit realm, thereby allowing them to see the soul of another. Needless to say, this argument has virtually no basis in Biblical tradition, rather it is comprised of the conjectures and beliefs of certain individuals.

Arguments suggesting reading auras is perfectly safe

Fortunately, there are several arguments that suggest the reading auras is actually safe and a non-issue with regards to sin. First and foremost of this is the fact that auras are commonly associated with positive figures in the Bible. There are no references to the devil having an aura, or of demons or bad people possessing them. Instead, those who are in close communion with God are seen as having auras, otherwise referred to as the "glory of God". Since auras are equated with God's glory, they are seen as something worth seeing, not something to be afraid of or to dismiss as unreal. In fact, several Biblical passages can be interpreted in such a way as to suggest that seeing auras is the result of positive personal development. One such example is the common theme of needing to be born again in order to see the Kingdom of God. While some interpret the "Kingdom of God" as Heaven, and thus the afterlife, others see it as the spirit realm. Therefore, a person who is born again should be able to see auras as they are, in theory, a very important part of the spirit realm.

Another argument for auras being healthy and safe is that people who were anointed by God or the Holy Spirit would be seen to "glow" as a result. This suggests that auras are a direct consequence of God's presence. Therefore, to see auras is to see the essence of God himself. No Christian would argue that this is a bad thing. Furthermore, when a person became closer to God in the Bible, they were likely to see otherworldly things and events, such as angels, future events and even the realms of Heaven and Hell. Therefore, being able to see such things is as much a result of being pure and holy as it is anything else.

Perhaps the most important thing to consider is the reason for wanting to see auras in the first place. After all, what makes an act good or bad often comes down to the intention behind the act. If you want to see someone's aura in order to help them, to know if they are safe, or for some other innocuous reason, then the action will be seen as equally innocuous. However, if you want to see auras for a more sinister reason, such as being able to see into another person for the sake of manipulating them, taking advantage of them or some other harmful reason then the act would become negative and harmful as a result. Therefore, what it really comes down to is the reason behind the action, not just the action itself. As long as your heart is right, your actions will be right as well.

The bottom line

Unfortunately, there is no general consensus regarding whether or not reading auras is right for Christians. However, that's not to say that both arguments are equally valid. As mentioned earlier, most of the arguments against reading auras revolve around the laws prohibiting such things as fortune telling, conjuring spirits and other such spiritual practices that reflect witchcraft, divination and the like. Reading auras is not any of these things as it doesn't attempt to see the future, associate with spirits or do anything else that could be seen as dabbling in spiritualism. Instead, reading auras is something that can be seen as natural and healthy, allowing a person to discern another person's health, state of mind and overall nature.

Another thing to consider is where the line is drawn between reading auras being a sin and reading auras being safe. Almost without exception, those arguments against reading auras come from traditions that are either more extreme in nature or those less based on Biblical verse and more based on personal belief and superstition. The traditions that state the reading auras is of the devil are the same traditions that said rock and roll was of the devil, that flying in planes was dabbling in spiritualism and other such bizarre things. While we may scoff at the quote "If God intended for man to fly, He would have given him wings!", the truth of the matter is that many a pastor in rural churches said as much when air travel was in its infancy. We know today that air travel is more about science and less about spirituality; therefore you won't go to hell if you book a seat on Delta. Likewise, the fact that auras have their place in science points to a future when they become as commonplace as air travel, rock and roll music and all the other phenomena and inventions that were sure to end humanity and cast us all to hell.

That said, it is up to you to make the decision as to whether reading auras is right for you. You should never do anything that makes you feel uncomfortable, no matter what it is. However, when it comes to finding actual Biblical quotes or passages to suggest that the reading of auras is a sin, none exist. Therefore, there is no factual reason to fear that auras and the reading of auras is anything but a natural extension of the human experience.

Part 3: Reading Auras

Chapter 7: Why Would Anyone Want to See Auras?

Now that you have a clear understanding of what auras are and their spiritual significance it is time to ask the next important question—why would anyone want to see auras in the first place? This is an important question to answer as it will establish a sense of purpose when learning the techniques required for seeing and reading auras. Furthermore, when you have a good reason for pursuing this goal you can decide that your reasons outweigh any concerns you might have regarding the correctness of seeing and reading auras. As mentioned earlier, what makes anything right or wrong usually comes down to the intention behind the action. Thus, once you determine that your intentions are wholesome, you can proceed with a clear conscience. Below are some of the most common ways in which the practice of reading auras can be used to improve your life, health, and overall wellbeing.

Application in day-to-day life

Despite the fact the origin and nature of auras are disputed by different religious and scientific circles, there are many things that both sides do actually agree upon. One of the most important of these agreements is the idea that an aura can tell you a lot about the person it belongs to. The fact is that a person's aura is a bit like a window into their soul or mind. When you are able to see their aura, you are able to see through the veil of physical appearance. As well as any 'deceptive' measures they might take such as the words they say, the image they project or any other element that might be used to trick you into believing a person is one thing when in fact they are something different altogether. Therefore, seeing a person's aura can help you to spot a dangerous person before they have a chance to try to work their charms on you.

Another way that reading auras can be beneficial is in the event that you are interviewing someone for a job. Needless to say, anyone that goes on an interview will practice their answers in the hopes of telling you exactly what you want to hear so that you will hire them. The problem with this is that you can never truly tell when a person is being honest and when they are deceiving you. This is because everyone you interview will be deceiving you to some degree. However, when you can read someone's aura, you can tell instantly whether they are trustworthy or not. Therefore, the ability to read auras can give you a real advantage when it comes to deciding who to hire for your company. Now you can discover a person's "true colors" long before they can cause any harm.

Keeping you safe

The ability to read auras can be very beneficial for general safety when you are walking around in public places. In the event that you find yourself alone with strangers, such as in a parking garage, an elevator or some other common public environment, being able to read auras can give you a real edge. Most people have to assume that the people they find themselves among are trustworthy and safe. Unfortunately, that theory doesn't always prove true. However, when you can read auras, you can determine the mindset of the people around you. Now, rather than hoping for the best you can rest assured that the people in the elevator are safe or the person in the parking garage means no harm. Alternatively, when you read another person's aura, you might discover an inherent danger. Fortunately, by reading their aura you will give yourself time to avoid the person, thereby keeping yourself safe in the process.

Reading auras can also serve to keep you safe when it comes to relationships. All too often people change once you get into a very serious relationship with them. It can seem as though they only tried to do the right thing for as long as it took to get you to commit to them. Once committed, things can often change for the worse. This is especially true when you consider that a significant percentage of violent crimes are committed by people close to the victim. Fortunately, when you have the ability to read auras you can discover a person's true nature in time to keep from putting yourself in any real danger. Now, despite how smooth talking or charming a person may appear to be you can see their true intentions. Needless to say, no one could ever argue against learning how to read auras when this is one of the benefits you can achieve by doing so.

A source of self-awareness

When you think about reading auras you probably think about reading other people's auras. While this is the usual practice, the fact of the matter is that you can also develop the ability to read your own aura. This can have a great many applications, all of which are highly beneficial to you and your overall wellbeing. The first way that reading your aura can help you is auras can warn a person of illness even before any physical symptoms appear. Since the ability to treat or even cure an illness is based on the stage in which the illness is detected this can have seriously positive ramifications. By keeping a regular eye on the nature of your aura you can tell just how healthy you are in body and mind. The moment you see a change for the worse you can take steps to prevent the oncoming illness that the vast majority of people simply aren't able to do.

In addition to telling you about your physical wellbeing, auras can tell you a great deal about the wellbeing of your mind and soul as well. This can come in real handy for anyone who suffers from such things as panic attacks, depression and other conditions that can make life difficult. By keeping an eye on the state of your aura, you can see the onset of any such condition in time to prevent the full effect of the symptoms. If you see that you are approaching a depressed state of mind, you can take the time to get out of the house and do something fun. Alternatively, if you detect heightened anxiety, you can give yourself some quiet time in which you can recharge your batteries and avoid the stress and anxiety that would have consumed you otherwise. In a way, seeing auras is a bit like being able to see around the corner before actually turning the corner. You can see if something dangerous is lurking, like depression or anxiety, and avoid it by going a different way. This can give you a level of control over your life that most never even dream of having.

Identifying health issues

Reading auras can also allow you to see the physical, emotional and mental health and wellbeing of another person. For example, if a person's aura is dull, it can signify that they are fatigued or depressed. Certain colors can represent general illnesses in a person, even before physical symptoms have begun to appear. Furthermore, a bright aura may represent that a person is deep in thought, engaged in a creative process, or using their minds in some other way that increases their energy levels accordingly.

Knowing how to read auras can help you to identify issues that another person might be suffering from. In the case where you know the person well you might be able to recommend that they get a checkup in order to identify any illness that their aura is indicating. Alternatively, if you notice that their aura seems fatigued or depressed, you can suggest that they get some rest to restore their energy levels, or perhaps get out and do something fun in order to shake off any sad or depressed feelings. Needless to say, being able to read a person's aura doesn't make you a doctor. This isn't about diagnosing a person and recommending treatment. Rather, reading a person's aura gives you the opportunity to increase their awareness of how they feel and if they need to take action in order to improve their overall health and wellbeing.

Gaining a deeper understanding of life

Finally, there is the aspect of gaining a deeper understanding of life by being able to see and read auras. While the science and details of auras and their meanings is of great importance, what is possibly of greater importance is the simple fact that auras exist at all. For thousands of years, humanity has established one spiritual tradition after another in the quest of answering some of life's most fundamental questions. One such question is the existence of the immortal soul. While being able to see auras might not actually provide proof to this age-old question it can give you a sense of hope and belief that so many others will never have. Once you begin seeing auras, you will never again doubt that there is more to life than meets the eye. This will give you a whole new perspective on things, something that no one can ever take away.

Another thing that the ability to see and read auras can give you is a sense of belonging. All too often people tend to feel isolated and alone in life. This is usually due to the fact that our physical bodies serve to separate us from everything that surrounds us. Eventually, this sense of separation can make a person feel distant from everyone and everything they come into contact with. However, once you begin to see auras, you will discover that all things possess energy of one form or another. This opens your eyes to the fact that all things are a living part of the reality you find yourself in. Once you see this shared essence of energy, you will begin to feel a part of the big picture in a way you may never have imagined possible. This is one of the biggest reasons why reading auras is a significant practice in many mystical religious traditions. When you see the soul of all things, you begin to awaken to a whole new understanding of life.

Chapter 8: Can Anyone Read Auras?

One of the most important questions raised with regard to auras is that if they exist, why can't everyone see them? This question is hotly debated within both scientific and religious circles to this very day. While there is more than enough evidence to support the fact that auras exist too little is known about how some people are able to see them. As a result, some scientists claim that auras can't be seen with the naked eye, and the people that claim to see them either have a physical condition, or they are simply making a false claim. Furthermore, not every religious tradition believes that everyone has the ability to see auras. Instead, several schools of thought claim that only spiritually developed people have the gift, while others claim it is a gift bestowed by God himself. Based on these arguments you could be forgiven for giving up trying to read auras even before you got started.

Fortunately, there is another side to this coin. That side states that the ability is present in everyone. It simply needs to be discovered and nurtured. One way to understand this approach is to think of it in terms of playing the piano. You wouldn't argue whether or not pianos exist based on whether or not everyone can play one. While a prodigy will pop up from time to time with an inherent ability, most people can only play the piano after years of arduous classes and recitals. Furthermore, each person's ability is based on their inherent talent coupled with their desire to learn and improve. This dynamic exists in many different forms, including such things as cooking, flying airplanes, driving a car or even baking cookies. No one wakes up one morning with a special gift that allows them to open the oven door and create magical cookies from scratch. You have to find the recipe, get the ingredients and follow the directions. According to this argument, reading auras is no different. As long as you put in the effort, you will achieve the results.

Learning to strengthen your senses

The biggest argument against a person being able to see or read auras is how can the human eye be trained to see beyond the visible light spectrum? While this argument may seem pretty water-tight at first, it is in fact fairly feeble. On the one hand, there is no real reason to assume that an aura consists of light beyond the visible spectrum. Unless the light created is in the ultra-violet or infrared spectrums it would be visible. That's not to suggest that it will be easy to see, simply that it would be *possible* to see. Therefore, it is important to avoid jumping to any conclusions regarding the light of an aura being invisible to the naked eye. No one has actually measured the light in terms of spectrum, so there is as much reason to believe it's visible as there is to believe that it isn't.

On the other hand, the fact is that the senses can be honed in a way so as to allow a person to do things that would be generally believed to be impossible. One example of this can be seen in lifting heavy objects. Numerous accounts exist that tell of instances where a person was able to lift far more than they should have been capable of in extreme circumstances. From mothers lifting a car off of their child to people lifting tree limbs off of a friend, many stories of "superhuman" strength can be found and validated. While this isn't the same thing as seeing an aura, it is nevertheless an example of seemingly impossible things being achieved.

Honing the senses doesn't have to be superhuman in nature. In fact, many people experience this phenomenon in their regular day-to-day lives. Any time you find yourself in a new environment where you have to learn new skills and develop different abilities, it can seem all but impossible at first. However, over time you find that your senses adapt to your environment and before you know it those things that seemed impossible at first become second nature. A job might require you to respond to sounds that you find difficult to discern at first, or it might require you to see things that are all but invisible to the average person. In time as you train your senses to "tune in" to these things, you develop the ability to hear more and see more than you did before. Developing your senses to see auras is absolutely the same thing. Therefore, it can be done.

Opening your third eye

This developing of the senses to perceive the aura is what is referred to in certain spiritual circles as the opening of the third eye. According to these traditions, every person has a spiritual "eye" that can see into non-physical reality. This is why some people can foretell future events, read other people's emotions, see current events unfolding halfway around the world and do other such inexplicable feats. The basic belief is that every person has the same senses in both the physical and spiritual realms. Thus, just as you can see, hear and touch tangible items in regular day-to-day reality, you can see, hear and touch things in the spirit realm as well. At first, this might seem beyond belief, but the truth is that you are probably experiencing some of this without even realizing it.

Perhaps the best example of a person "seeing" into the non-physical realm is when a person dreams. Although some people might argue that dreams are nothing more than images that process events, emotions, and memories from the previous day they are nonetheless a non-physical reality in which an individual can see, hear and touch just like they can in regular life. Additionally, countless case files exist telling of times when a person dreamt of an event that later took place, received a message from a loved one long since departed, or some other phenomenon that simply cannot be explained in a rational way. Many spiritual traditions see the dream state as an otherworldly experience, one that is equally real and vital as the physical reality we focus so much of our time and effort on. The bottom line is that such traditions would see dreams as an example of seeing beyond normal reality. Thus, anyone who can dream can learn to see auras with a little time, effort and practice.

While some spiritual traditions believe that seeing auras can only be achieved by opening and training the third eye others believe that it's simply a matter of not paying so much attention to physical reality. In other words, rather than having to develop a whole new way of seeing you only have to tune out what your physical senses are telling you and listen to what your non-physical senses are trying to say. This is a bit like when someone closes their eyes in order to listen more intently to a sound. It is a fact that when you close your eyes, your brain will focus more on the other senses as it no longer has to process what you see. This is why blind people have more acute hearing. It's not that they develop their hearing more, it's simply that their brain focuses more energy on the other senses and interpreting the information those senses provide. Subsequently, when you pay less attention to your physical senses you are able to pick up on the information your spiritual senses are sending you. Therefore, learning to see auras can be as simple as learning to ignore your physical sight and allow your spiritual sight to "kick in".

The power of the mind

In the end what it really comes down to is the power of the mind. Whether you believe that seeing and reading auras is something that is superhuman or whether you believe it's something fairly straightforward the bottom line is that you have to believe. The stronger your faith in the process is the stronger and faster your results will be. Just as a person who believes they can lose weight or run faster or meet the person of their dreams will be more likely to achieve their goal than someone who doesn't believe, so too, you will only struggle in this process if you allow doubt and skepticism to set in. Everything you do in life is as easy or as hard as you perceive it to be. Therefore, it is critical that you set your mind to accepting the fact that you can and will see auras without any trouble or much effort on your part. Once you establish that fact in your mind you will be able to turn it into a reality.

Furthermore, if you can envision your success you will be more likely to achieve it. Imagination can play a crucial role in being able to see and read auras. Just as dreaming about winning an Olympic medal motivates an athlete to train day after day, so too, seeing yourself reading auras like a pro can help you to stay on track with your daily efforts and practice. Your imagination can also help you to open up to seeing beyond your normal spectrum. When you envision what it will be like to see an aura you will give yourself something to look for, and this can make all the difference. If you feel lost and confused, it may take longer to get significant results. However, if you imagine those results, you will open your mind to the possibility in a whole new way. After all, most of what you do in your life begins as a thought, dream or idea. Developing your ability to see and read auras should be approached in exactly the same way.

Chapter 9: Simple Steps for Activating Your Aura Reading Ability

Now that you know what auras are, who has one and who can read them it's time to address the actual practice of seeing auras. Fortunately, learning the methods for seeing auras is fairly easy and straightforward. The fact of the matter is that there are only a few methods commonly used. Therefore, the majority of your time and effort will be spent on perfecting the process rather than learning many different techniques. Furthermore, once you find a method that works for you, there is no need to try other ones. Instead, it is recommended that you spend your time and energy improving your technique, tweaking it to suit your personal abilities so that it becomes second nature. Once you take ownership of your ability and the technique you use there will be no limit to what you can achieve.

Get the feel of it

The first step toward seeing and reading auras doesn't even

utilize your vision, physical or otherwise. Instead, the first step is to feel the energy of a person, place or thing. This may seem counterintuitive at first, but the truth is that it becomes much easier to see energy once you have developed the ability to feel it. This method is about combining your senses to achieve your goal. By using multiple senses you can "perceive" an aura with greater intensity than if you relied on a single sense alone.

Learning to feel energy is actually a very simple process. Many people already possess this ability to some degree, making it more a matter of developing your sense rather than actually discovering it. You can start with more extreme scenarios, such as public events. A sporting event, for example, will contain a great deal of excited and anxious energy. The chances are you can't help but feel that energy when you are in a stadium surrounded by thousands of people. That's what makes this a great place to start. By letting yourself feel the energy of the people and the moment you can become familiar with how that energy feels. Pay attention to specific ways in which the energy affects you, such as making the hair on your arms and neck stand up, giving you goosebumps, overwhelming your senses or some other physiological effect. Once you identify these effects, you can use them to detect heightened energy under more normal circumstances.

Another way you can practice feeling energy is to focus on how you feel when you are around someone who is experiencing heightened emotions. Rather than avoiding someone who is visibly angry, take the opportunity to see how the air around that person feels. You don't have to get in the persons face to do this, simply place yourself a few feet away and see how their energy makes you feel. Once you get a sense of how to feel another person's energy you are well on your way to being able to see that energy. In a way, this is a bit like smelling something before you taste it. By breathing in the essence of a hot, tasty beverage you give yourself an idea of how it will taste before drinking it. This enhances the flavor once you do take a sip, making the experience that much more impactful. This is how combining your senses to increase your perception of a thing works. Being able to feel energy will help you to see an aura more easily and clearly.

Start small

When starting any venture, it is always smart to start small and work your way up to the more complicated and difficult aspects later. The same principle applies to seeing and reading auras. Since the auras of people are fairly complex, being comprised of multiple layers, colors, and other variables, it is a good idea to leave them for later. When starting, you should try to see auras that are less complex and potentially easier to see. Plants can provide the perfect solution for this approach. One reason why reading plants is a good way to start is that plants have a simple aura, consisting of a single layer that is of a white or yellow color. Since plants lack the complex thoughts and emotions of humans they also lack the various colors and layers of human auras. Therefore, all you have to do is try to see the light that surrounds a plant, which is pretty straightforward.

Another reason why plants prove to be good for beginners is that they are stationary. This means you can sit and stare at a plant for as long as you need to without the plant getting bored and wandering off. Furthermore, the plant won't create any distraction. This will allow you to remain focused on reading the plant's aura without losing concentration due to movement, conversation or any other potentially distracting action. Additionally, you can use a plant any time day or night, which means you can practice whenever you want. This can be of significant importance since many people find that they get better results when they feel inspired to practice. By using a plant, you can ensure that you have a willing "partner" for those times when you feel particularly inspired.

Practice with neutral backgrounds

Now that you have a reliable partner to practice with the next thing to do is to create the right environment. Ordinarily, you should use a wall that is painted in a neutral color, such as beige, off-white or some other "non-color" as the background. The more neutral the color of the background is the easier it will be to see the aura of the subject. However, since plants don't have colors in their auras you can choose to use a darker background in this case. A black wall would actually be perfect as any low-level light would be easy to detect against such a backdrop. Since plants have a lower intensity aura it can be harder to see their auras against lighter colors.

Another important factor regarding your practice environment is the lighting in the room. Ideally, you should have a room with low lighting, as this will help you to see the light of an aura. Daylight is not recommended, as it can prove both bright and changeable. The last thing you need is to have the light of the room change with each passing cloud. Furthermore, any shadows cast by birds flying by will only create a distraction, which will make your practice more difficult as a result. Therefore, a room with no windows is preferable, like a bathroom or even a closet. Pitch black isn't recommended, however, as you want to be able to see your subject in order to see their aura. Something else to consider is the time of day you choose to practice in. Evening hours can be ideal as any room, windowed or otherwise, will have little to no outside light coming in. This will help you to gain control over the lighting of the room, which will help you to get better results.

Use indirect vision

The next step is to start looking for that ever-elusive aura! In addition to using the right lighting and background, it is important to create the right distance between you and your subject. The general rule of thumb is that you should be no further away than two feet and no closer than one foot from the person or plant you want to read. How far away you are from your subject may seem irrelevant, but it can actually make all the difference, especially when you are a beginner. If you are too close to your subject, you won't be able to see their surrounding space. Since this is where their aura is located this means you are reducing your line of sight, making it harder to achieve results. Alternatively, if you are too far away, you might become distracted by other objects in the room. Since your mind is programmed to take in any and all visual information, the more you offer it, the more it will accept. Thus, if you have furniture or other objects in the room, you will struggle to keep them tuned out if you are further away from the person you are trying to read. By establishing the right distance, you will ensure that your field of vision contains only the subject and the surrounding area around them.

Once you have everything set up the next step is to look at your subject. At first, you might be tempted to actually look at their head or face, but this isn't where you want to focus your attention. As mentioned earlier, the aura of a person or object *surrounds* them; therefore you want to focus your attention on the area just above the head. In the case of a plant, you can focus your attention an inch or so above the highest part of the plant. One way to understand this is to think of the shimmering effect of heat on an object. Just as extreme heat can cause the air over an object to shimmer, creating a wavy effect that surrounds the object, so too, an aura creates a similar effect. However, instead of shimmering heat, the aura creates shimmering light. The important thing is that in order to see the aura you look just over the subject, just as you would look over an object to see the heat effect.

Another important thing to consider when looking at your subject is that you want to relax your eyes, virtually allowing them to go out of focus. Subtle light is harder to see when you are staring at it with clear, focused eyes. This can be demonstrated when you look at the night sky. Sometimes the fainter stars will only be visible when you look to the left or the right of them. When you look directly at them, they seem to disappear. That is how subtle light works. Your peripheral vision can pick up on such low-level light far better than your focused vision can. Therefore, either you can let your eyes go out of focus a bit, or you can choose to look to the side of your subject the same way you would cast your sight to the side of a faint star in order to perceive it.

The question most people ask at this point is exactly how long you have to hold this pose. Many people associate seeing auras with meditation as they both have similarly spiritual overtones. However, unlike with meditation, you only have to hold this pose for between half a minute and a full minute. Seeing an aura is exactly like seeing that faint star in the night sky. You don't have to stare at the sky for hour after hour in order to see it; instead you just have to shift your focus and allow yourself to see it. In the end, this takes only seconds to do. It can take a minute or so in the case of an aura, but it shouldn't take more than that. If you don't see some indication of an aura in that time the chances are your environment is not quite right. There may be too much light, too much distraction or maybe your distance isn't what it needs to be. In this case, you should try changing the different elements in order to find the right combination. After you make a change try reading the aura again, but only spend up to a minute each time. Eventually, you will see the aura, so don't give up!

Practicing on yourself

Once you have had your first glimpse of an aura, whether it's from a plant, your pet or a person, you can begin to practice reading auras on yourself. This can have many advantages as you will prove a very willing and patient partner to work with! Additionally, you will always be available when you feel the urge to practice. Perhaps the biggest advantage to practicing on yourself is that you can begin to develop your ability to see more complex auras this way. When you are able to see layers, brightness, and colors in your aura you will be able to see the same in other people and objects with greater ease and clarity.

The best way to practice reading your own aura is to read the aura around your hands. This practice will ensure that you are the right distance away from the subject, that your field of vision is right and that there is little to no distraction to undermine your concentration. Remove any jewelry from your hand in order to eliminate anything that could prove distracting. A good trick to enhance the results is to rub your hands together briskly before reading them. This will excite the energy around your hands, making it brighter and thus easier to see. It is important to ensure that you use the right environment when performing this task as the lighting, background color and other variables are just as relevant when reading yourself as they are when reading another subject.

Another variation of reading your aura is what is known as the mirror method. This has you sit in front of a mirror and read the aura around your reflection. Since any light is reflected in a mirror, this won't be any more difficult than reading an aura directly. Again, make sure that the environmental conditions are right, including the distance between you and the mirror. Allow your eyes to go slightly out of focus, or focus on something just above or to the side of you and give it a minute. You will begin to see a shimmering light surrounding your shape, as though you were looking at a double exposed image. Once you see your aura try to notice specific details about it, including brightness, color, whether it is calm or agitated and any other aspects that might contain valuable information. Your first attempts may provide few to no results, but with practice, you will begin to see your aura more easily and more clearly, leading to you being able to tap into your ability virtually anytime and anywhere.

A final thought

The fact of the matter is that reading auras is easier for some people than it is for others. While there is no definitive reason for this, there are a few factors that do seem to play a significant part in the process. Perhaps the most important thing to remember is that you need to allow the process to happen. More often than not those who have a hard time seeing auras are the ones who try to make it happen. The more you try to force the situation is the less likely you are to achieve any meaningful results. Alternatively, when you surrender yourself to the process, you will be almost guaranteed to achieve the results you desire. In a way, it's a bit like listening to music. If you focus on the song you are listening to you will likely fixate on a particular element of the song. You might hear the lyrics more clearly, or you might hear a particular part of the music more clearly. In the end, the fact is that the more you focus on the music, the less you actually hear. In contrast, if you simply open your ears and mind to the song you are listening to you will find that you hear the whole song, lyrics, music and everything else. When you surrender to the song, your experience is richer, more meaningful and more satisfying. This is the way you need to approach reading auras. Don't become fixated on a particular feature of the practice. Instead, open your heart and mind and allow the experience to find you.

Chapter 10: Once the Ability is Activated, Can it be Turned Off?

A common concern among those wanting to develop the skill of seeing auras is whether or not the ability is permanent. In other words, once the ability is activated can it be turned off? It is pretty ironic that the two main concerns regarding reading auras are whether it can be done and whether it can be undone! Still, the question regarding whether the ability can be turned off makes a lot of sense. After all, you don't necessarily want to always know the deep dark secrets of those around you. Furthermore, you might just want to go out and have a good time every now and then without having to deal with the nature of people's intentions, their health, and wellbeing or any other spiritual aspect regarding the rest of humanity. Fortunately, even though the reality of reading auras differs from person to person, the general consensus is that the ability can be both turned on and turned off largely at will. This chapter will address how your ability isn't something that will take over your life, rather it is something, which will be there for you to use at your discretion.

Tuning out

As mentioned earlier in this book, reading auras is an ability that comes to many when they learn to tune out their other senses. The reason why so many never learn to see or read auras is that they never filter out the information being received from their physical sight, hearing and other senses. Therefore, their minds are too busy dealing with physical sensory input to be able to grasp anything else. Only when a person is able to "blur" their physical senses can they begin to focus on their other senses, such as the ability to see and read auras.

The importance of this fact is that it can work in the other direction as well. Just as you have to tune out to your physical senses to be able to perceive auras, so too, if you want to tune out of seeing auras you simply have to re-focus on your physical senses once again. In other words, if you want to stop seeing with your "spiritual eyes" you need to simply focus on seeing with your physical eyes. Since you are more conditioned to paying attention to your physical sight in the first place, this practice won't be hard to master at all. In fact, you will probably find that you have to "turn on" your ability to see auras each and every time. It's highly unlikely that you will wake up and start your day seeing the auras of those around you. That's just not how it works.

However, assuming that you are that single exception to the rule, there is an easy way to rewire your brain so that it starts focusing on the physical rather than the spiritual. Simply put, all you need to do is to overwhelm your brain with physical sensory input. This doesn't have to be restricted to visual input; instead, it can be any sensory input at all. Thus, if you are somehow stuck on seeing auras, you can put some headphones on and crank up some music to flood your mind.

Once your brain clicks over to processing physical sensory input again, you will be free from seeing auras or any other extrasensory experiences. While no real reports have come forward of people being stuck in "aura mode" there are instances where people who are highly empathic have trouble distancing themselves from the thoughts and emotions of those around them. This technique of overwhelming the brain with physical sensory input is one of the most effective ways of switching off their empathic receptors and tuning into their own emotions once again.

Ongoing training

Another thing to consider is that seeing and reading auras is not like turning on a light switch. While there may be some people who are more naturally adept at the skill more often than not, it takes a great deal of training and practice in order to achieve meaningful results. Therefore, the notion that you are going to flip a switch that cannot be turned off once it's turned on is not realistic at all. Instead, you will probably find that you will have to focus some effort and energy into turning the ability on each and every time.

The idea that seeing and reading auras is something that requires effort and practice should not be seen as a negative. On the contrary, the effort required to achieve this skill is well worth it in the end. The reason for this is not only is the ability to read auras worth the time and effort invested, but you will find that you develop a great deal more in the process. While reading auras is a distinct skill, it is a part of a bigger non-physical world that we all live in. Therefore, as you develop your ability to see auras you will be developing your non-physical senses overall. Thus, you will find that your outlook on life begins to evolve during this process, giving you a whole new perspective on your sense of self, your perception of others and your understanding of life in general. As a result, you won't end up with just a neat trick that can get laughs at a party; rather you will end up with a strength that helps you to live a better and more meaningful life in many ways.

Additionally, you should realize that your training will be constant and ongoing. Since reading auras is a very complex ability, one that will change your life and potentially the lives of those around you, it will require continuous development and refining. You will find that you will want to hone your skills and improve your abilities for different reasons along the way. This will not only give you the ability to see and understand more, but it will also provide you with greater control over your gift. The more you train, the stronger you will become. Therefore, it's not like learning to fire a gun in the sense that a loaded gun is a dangerous thing. Instead, it's more like learning how to fight with a sword. Only when you become proficient will the sword become effective. In this way your gift will never dominate you, instead, you will be in constant control of it.

Not an open floodgate

Finally, it is important to understand that developing your extrasensory skills in any way is never like opening a floodgate. You don't have a dam inside of you holding back all sorts of psychic and spiritual energy waiting to be released. What you do have is spiritual muscles waiting to be trained and developed, just like physical muscles. No one has ever gone to the gym for a couple of weeks and come out looking like a bodybuilder. It takes years of hard work and discipline to achieve such results. Equally true, it takes years of hard work and discipline to achieve extraordinary results in psychic abilities. However, everyone can develop their common abilities with moderate effort and discipline, just as everyone can develop a decent physique with the same moderate effort and discipline. Subsequently, reading auras is not an all or nothing scenario. Instead, it is an ongoing progression of effort, practice, and experience.

Chapter 11: How to Interpret the Colors, Brightness, and Layers of Auras

Now that you have learned how to read auras it is time to discover what the different colors, brightness, and vibrations actually mean. The truth is that no two auras are exactly alike; therefore it is important to be able to understand the information they contain. Different colors can tell you a lot about the nature of a person or whether or not they are healthy and happy. Additionally, a bright aura will suggest one thing, whereas a dull aura will suggest something else. Therefore, once you are able to see auras it is vital that you begin to learn their language so that you can make sense of the wonderful things you are seeing. The colors, brightness, and vibrations of auras, along with their meanings, are listed below.

The ten colors of the aura

The number of colors found in the aura differs depending on which tradition you follow. Some traditions believe that as many as 12 colors exist, while others state that as few as three colors can be found. Overall, there is a general consensus on 10 basic colors, and that is what this section will discuss. Each of the 10 colors represents a different aspect of a person's character, health or overall wellbeing. Learning what each color means will take time and practice as there can be subtle variations of meaning depending on the person you are reading. The following are basic definitions of the 10 colors of the aura:

- **Red/pink-** When a person's aura is red or pink in color, it represents passion. Some suggest that red is the color of anger, but this can be a bit misleading. Anger or pent-up frustration will reveal itself as a dull or dirty red, whereas bright red indicates heightened passion. Thus, if a person has a red aura, they are simply likely to be highly passionate about life and the things they do. Therefore, a red aura doesn't have to be seen as dangerous or bad; rather it can be seen as a sign of passionate or eager energy.

- **Orange-** The color orange is associated with creativity and imagination. Therefore, if you see an orange aura around a person, you can assume that they are artistic, musical or literary in nature. Such people will usually be found in more creative environments such as museums, music stores, bookstores or the like. Furthermore, any person engaged in a creative activity will possess a more orange aura due to the nature of their experience at that particular moment. Another side of an orange aura is expressiveness and a desire to embrace life. Since these are attributes of more artistic and creative types, this makes sense.

- **Yellow-** A person with a yellow aura is someone who is generally optimistic and innocent in nature. They will often reflect a child-like tendency for simple pleasures and innocent fun, preferring laughter over serious conversation. When the color is clear and bright the person is enjoying life; however, when the color becomes diminished or dirty, it suggests that they are struggling with issues that are bringing them down. Ordinarily, such times will be short, and it will only take a little laughter before the bright yellow color of their aura is restored.

- **Green-** A green aura usually depicts growth, freshness and a general sense of health and wellbeing. Just as green in nature represents health and vitality, so too, a green aura suggests the very same thing. Someone with a green aura may be experiencing growth in their personal life, their spiritual life or any other aspect of their reality. Alternatively, such an aura may indicate that the individual has the power to bring health and vitality to others. Furthermore, they may be ideal at bringing fresh insights into a project or endeavor. A dull or dirty green aura, however, may indicate stagnation or greed. Unlike other dull colors, this may be less temporal, indicating an element of personality rather than temporary conditions.

- **Blue-** When a person has a blue aura, it indicates that they are in tune with those around them. Empaths are a prime example of blue aura people. Capable of not only connecting to others, but empaths can also help to remove suffering and restore happiness and strength to those going through hard times. The chances are that someone with a blue aura is just as capable of reading you as you are of reading them, so don't be surprised if they seem to know what you are doing! Even so, they won't be offended by it, so you won't have anything to worry about.

- **Indigo/dark blue-** An indigo or dark blue aura suggests that the person you are reading is deeply spiritual. This color is associated with the third eye, and as such represents spiritual awakening and insight. You won't find an indigo aura around the average person. Instead, such auras will only be found around those who devote their lives to understanding the nature of life, the role of the individual and such things as the soul, the afterlife and other such supernatural mysteries. The bottom line is that you will be able to recognize this type of person even before you read their aura.

- **Purple/violet-** The purple aura is connected to the crown chakra, and represents a deep connection with the Universe. While dark blue auras are associated with individuals seeking answers, purple auras are associated with individuals who have the answers. Rather than being seekers, a person with a purple aura will usually be a teacher, showing others the way to wisdom, insight and spiritual awakening. The brighter this color is, the more enlightened the individual is.

- **Silver-** A silver aura is one that will be fairly rare, as it represents those who are connected to the collective unconscious. Someone with this color aura will usually be very intuitive and compassionate, demonstrating a genuine love for humanity and all other living things. They will be very understanding of any situation and be able to relate to the thoughts and emotions of all involved. Such a person will seem less individualistic and more a part of the bigger picture. However, in the case that the aura is a dull silver or gray, this could indicate health issues, specifically in the area where the color is most present.

- **Gold-** Gold auras represent an almost otherworldly quality to the individual. Being that they are associated with great spiritual maturity, these auras are very rare and unique. More often than not people with gold auras will devote their lives to serving humanity, especially those in dire need. They will also likely have removed themselves from the proverbial grid, neither needing money nor wanting the material things it can buy. A person with this color aura will be someone characterized by a sense of transcendence. Although they may be in this world, they are almost certainly not a part of it.

- **White-** Finally there is the color white. Many cultures identify white as the color of purity, truth, and holiness, and these are exactly the attributes that a white aura represents. Anyone with a white aura will be trustworthy, pure of heart and usually more focused on spiritual matters than matters of the physical plain of existence. Furthermore, such individuals will often possess the ability to bring health and strength to those they touch, be it in physical, mental or spiritual terms. All in all, if you see someone with a white aura you will have discovered a rare treasure.

The seven aura layers

As you develop your ability to see and read auras, you might begin to see different layers of a person's aura. Sometimes these different layers might surround the whole body; however, they usually project from certain areas of the body. This is because the different layers of the aura are directly connected to the seven chakras of the subtle body. As a result, there are seven layers or areas of an aura, each with its own importance and meaning. The seven aura layers are as follows:

- **Layer 1- the etheric body.** The first layer of the aura is the etheric body. Emanating from the root chakra, this layer represents the physical body in terms of health and wellbeing. It envelopes the physical body, sometimes appearing as a blurry layer much like when a camera goes out of focus. It is usually blue-gray in color and has a relatively smooth vibration rate. The etheric body is brighter and more distinct in people who are physically active, such as athletes, bodybuilders and the like. However, it is also brighter among those who are healthy and have strong energy levels. Weak or dull etheric bodies can indicate illness, fatigue or general poor health.

- **Layer 2- the emotional body.** The second layer of the aura is the emotional body. This layer signifies the emotional health and wellbeing of a person, just like the etheric body does for physical health and wellbeing. Emanating from the solar plexus chakra this layer has many colors, appearing like a layer of rainbow light surrounding the individual. When a person is feeling happy and emotionally strong, this layer is brighter and more pronounced. However, when a person is depressed, troubled or sad, this layer will become dull in both brightness and color. Since a person's emotional state has a profound impact on their overall health and wellbeing, the condition of this layer often determines the condition of the aura as a whole.

- **Layer 3- the mental body.** This layer of the aura is relatively close to the physical body, hovering a mere 2-3 inches away. It emanates from the sacral chakra and is associated with mental activity. When a person is deep in thought and concentration, this layer will appear more vibrant and distinct. Generally yellow in color, the mental body can appear quite chaotic at times, especially in those who have highly active minds and imaginations. In fact, it is reported that during highly creative activities a person's mental body can be seen to produce sparks, as though the energy was about to catch fire! Highly intelligent people will demonstrate strong mental bodies, while those less intellectually inclined will have duller, less vibrant mental bodies.

- **Layer 4- the astral body.** Radiating from the heart chakra, the fourth layer of the aura is known as the astral body. Located between 6 and 12 inches from the physical body, this is the layer that is most associated with spiritual practices such as lucid dreaming, astral projection and the like. Specifically tuned in to a person's relationships, the color and brightness of the astral body will intensify the more an individual experiences love and affection. It can appear weak and dim during such events as divorce, losing a loved one and any other relationship trauma. A healthy astral body will have a bright pink hue, whereas a damaged or weak astral body will have a dusty pink hue.

- **Layer 5- the etheric double.** The fifth layer of the aura, the etheric double, is located just over 1 foot above the physical body. It emanates from the throat chakra and represents a person's physical reality. Such things as a person's personality, identity, and their overall achievements are contained in this layer. Therefore, when a person is very active and self-aware, their etheric double will be brighter and more pronounced. However, if a person has low ambition, a low sense of self-esteem and doesn't achieve much this layer will be less defined. Usually, the etheric double is blue in color, although the specific color depends on the individual's physical reality.

- **Layer 6- the celestial body.** The celestial body is the sixth layer of the aura and is associated with the third eye or sixth chakra. It is located about 2 feet from the physical body, just above the etheric double. This layer responds to the level of enlightenment that an individual achieves. When a person is more enlightened, their celestial body will appear bright and white in color. Such a person will usually exhibit high levels of compassion and love for those around them, mirroring the divine love for all living things. They will also have greater awareness and a strong sense of purpose. However, when a person is less enlightened, their celestial body will be hard to see as it will be less developed and thus, possess less energy.

- **Layer 7- the ketheric template.** This final layer of the aura resides as far away as 2-3 feet from the physical body. It represents the relationship of the individual to the Universe as a whole and thus is related to the crown chakra. Characteristically this layer is gold in color; however, the brightness and clarity of the color will depend on the spiritual development of the individual. Those who are less spiritually evolved may not even demonstrate this layer of their aura at all. When this aura is strong the person will experience oneness with the Universe and all living things, and may even have recollections of past lives and numerous inherent spiritual abilities.

How to interpret the brightness and vibrations of an aura

In addition to having different colors, each aura will have its own brightness and frequency of vibration. These factors can tell a lot about the person, including their emotional condition, their overall health and whether or not they like you. The different meanings of an aura's brightness and vibration are as follows:

- **A bright aura.** As you might expect the brightness of a person's aura is directly related to their overall energy levels. Thus, a bright aura will indicate that the person has high energy levels. Since energy levels are directly influenced by the physical condition of a person, a high energy level, demonstrated by a bright aura, will suggest that the person is in good physical health.

  A bright aura will also suggest that the individual is in a good state of mind. When a person is happy, excited or amused, their energy levels will generally increase, creating a brighter aura as a result. Therefore, in addition to suggesting good physical health, a bright aura will also indicate good mental and emotional health and wellbeing.

- **A dull aura.** In contrast, a dull aura will suggest that the individual has low energy levels. This isn't necessarily a bad thing, however, as someone who is simply tired or fatigued can possess a dull aura for the time being. Once the person is rested their energy levels will be restored, creating a brighter aura as a result. Although, if a dull aura is persistent in a person it can point to something more significant. For some reason, the person's energy levels are chronically low, and this is usually the result of illness or poor physical health in general.

  Another cause of a dull aura can be low mental activity or depression. Just as high mental functions, including happiness, excitement and the like will produce a bright aura, low mental functions such as sadness, boredom and depression will have the opposite effect. Again, this condition may be temporary and simply point to the mood of the individual at that particular moment. However, if the dull aura is constant, then it will point to something more significant such as poor emotional or mental health.

- **A smooth aura.** When a person has a smooth aura it means that their energy is vibrating at a calm and steady rate. This can look like the surface of a lake or pond under a gentle breeze. The way that the water ripples gently and evenly is the way that an aura will "ripple" when it is smooth. Just as a lake has gentle ripples when the weather is calm, so too, a person's aura has gentle ripples when their mind is at peace. Thus, when you see a smooth aura you know that the person you are reading is relatively calm and content.

- **An excited aura.** If a person's aura appears more like an erratic light show, it signifies that they are anything but calm and content. The more chaotic the vibration of a person's aura is the more chaotic their emotions are. This can be the result of anger or rage, as these emotions will cause an aura to become highly energized and erratic in appearance. However, it can also point to less sinister emotions, such as anxiety, eagerness or anticipation. Basically, any emotion that isn't calm will create a lack of calmness in the aura.

Part 4: Using the Information Auras Reveal

Chapter 12: How to Deal with Disturbing Information

Being able to see and read auras can be an extraordinary experience. Just knowing that you are getting a glimpse into the world beyond physical senses is something that will change your life forever. Not only does it create a sense of wonder and awe every time you tap into your ability, but it also allows you to see people in a more meaningful way. Now you can see a person's true nature without even having to introduce yourself to them! Unfortunately, there is a darker side to this miracle that many discover unexpectedly. That side is when you see information that is disturbing in one way or another. It can be all fun and games to see the positive side of auras, but when you discover the negative side, it can be overwhelming and hard to cope with. In the end, it is critical that you have a plan for how to deal with disturbing information as you will experience this situation at one time or another. This chapter provides examples of different types of disturbing information as well as several techniques on how to deal with the information once it's there.

Dealing with illness

One of the most common pieces of information obtained by reading auras is a person's health and overall wellbeing. This isn't limited to physical health, however, but also encompasses mental, emotional and spiritual health as well. More often than not when you discover that a person is suffering from some illness or condition it is not something too significant, making it easy to deal with. However, there will be times when you discover a serious illness even before the person is aware of it themselves. This creates a situation where many people are left not knowing what to say or do, which makes them feel conflicted as a result. After all, if you don't tell the person what you know, then you feel responsible when their condition gets worse. Alternatively, what if you freak them out by telling them that you know they have a serious illness or disease? In the end, this can seem like a no-win situation, but the truth is that you can find a way to share the information so that the person can benefit from early detection of their illness.

The first thing to do is to avoid being too blunt with the person you are reading. If you discover that a person seems to have a life-threatening illness, the last thing you should do is scream "Oh my God you're going to die!" However, the second to last thing you should do is say nothing at all. Fortunately, there is a balance point in which you can serve the function of providing information without creating panic or other issues. All you need to do is present your information in a more natural way. Instead of trying to explain your ability to this person simply tell them that you are concerned with how they appear physically. Ask them if they have been to the doctor lately and suggest that they get a checkup. The chances are they will have some physical symptoms of one form or another since the aura won't be so far ahead of the body that the body would be completely symptom-free. Therefore, try to "translate" your findings into any physical symptoms that can be seen or felt. This will enable you to encourage your friend to seek medical attention in a natural and sincere way without creating any awkwardness or regret.

Unfortunately, there may be times when you see that a person is in a really bad way, so much so that there may not be anything that can be done to reverse the situation. This often happens when a person is undergoing treatment for a condition. Sometimes their symptoms may seem to clear up, giving them and their doctors hope that the treatment is working. However, this may only be an appearance, and the truth is that the condition is unaffected and still doing its damage. An aura will show this, even when physical symptoms seem to be improving. When you detect this the only thing you can do is accept that this person will probably not recover from their situation. While you might feel as though there is something you can do to change this, the chances are there isn't. The simple truth is all you can do in such a situation is make yourself available to the person and make sure your last moments with them are happy and full of good memories. Even though this may not seem like enough, it is far more than you would have been able to do otherwise. One thing you have to remember is just because you can read auras doesn't mean you can change the way things are. You simply see things in a new way; you don't necessarily control them.

When you detect deceit

Another form of disturbing news you might encounter when

reading an aura is deception. Unfortunately, there are many people out there who appear nice and charming but underneath the façade lies a person who is greedy, selfish and ready to take advantage of everyone they can. It can be all too easy to fall for the charms of such a person when you don't have any way of knowing their true intentions; however, when you can read their aura, you know exactly who they are and what they want. Fortunately, this can keep you from getting into a situation that costs you time, money and potentially a whole lot more. The trick is how to process this information in a way that keeps you safe without showing your hand in the process.

In the event that you know that someone is not to be trusted all you have to do is keep your distance from them as much as possible. Don't put yourself in a situation where they can take advantage of you, whether it's loaning them money, giving them a place to stay, or some other scenario that sees you giving freely to someone who will never give back. This doesn't mean that you can't talk to them or even become friends with them. In fact, just because someone's aura indicates that they are untrustworthy doesn't mean that they would necessarily do you any harm. All it means is that they are highly capable of doing so, and thus should be treated accordingly. Just as you take extra precautions with dangerous things, such as using mitts to remove a hot dish from the oven, so too, use extra caution when interacting with people who may "burn" you if you get too close.

There might be times when you want to share your insights with others to help them stay safe from those who would take advantage of them. This can be a tricky situation as more often than not deceitful people come across as very friendly, genuine and trustworthy. Trying to convince someone that they aren't as they seem cannot only be difficult, it can actually make you appear to be the bad guy in the situation. Therefore, a great deal of tact is necessary for such an undertaking. The most important thing to remember is that it's not up to you to make other people's decisions for them. Instead, simply give some friendly advice and let your friends do as they will. In the end, you will be proven to be right. From that moment on your advice will be more readily accepted and even sought after. So long as you don't try to force your opinion onto others, you will have done the right thing.

Avoiding danger

Perhaps the most important way in which aura information can prove useful is when it helps you to avoid danger. This can happen in many different ways and many different places. One such example would be if you found yourself in a relatively abandoned place by yourself. You might be going home from work later than normal, and the parking garage might be all but empty. As you walk to your car, you might find another person appear and start walking in your direction. Needless to say, this can be a time for concern. Fortunately, you can access your gift of reading auras and determine the true nature of the other person long before they become a threat. If their aura is peaceful and calm, you have nothing to worry about. However, if you see anger, chaos, and disturbance in their aura you know they should be avoided. Once you make this discovery, you should do everything you can to get to a safe place, even if it means leaving the garage and finding other people. You can always ask someone to walk you to your car later on. Of course you should make sure their aura is good before doing so!

Unfortunately, not all danger comes from strangers in dark places. All too often those close to us prove to be capable of things we would never have imagined. This is another way that reading auras can come in real handy. Long before you get into a relationship that could prove dangerous and destructive, you will be able to determine whether the other person is safe or not. This will help you to avoid danger in every way possible. Unfortunately, the same situation may arise when you know the truth about someone that could significantly impact someone else's life. In this case, you need to do the same thing as when sharing concerns about medical issues or deceptive people. Start by offering friendly advice that can help to keep the other person safe.

Additionally, look for "symptoms" that might reveal the person's true nature. If they have a short temper, or they act in an aggressive or hostile way to people you can use these behaviors as warning signs of something more sinister. This is the act of translating your information into information others can perceive. Once they begin to see the symptoms of dangerous behavior your advice will become more reasonable and sound. In the end, all you can do is try to help keep your friends and loved ones safe. You can't just take control of their lives because you know things they don't. Instead, you must content yourself with simply trying to steer them in a direction that is safer and happier. It is still up to them to make their choices. As long as you offer your advice, you will have done all you can. And even though it may not feel like it's enough, always remember that it's more than they would have had otherwise.

Chapter 13: Can Auras Change?

One question that is often asked is whether auras are permanent or if they are capable of changing. While there are several different approaches to this question, the simple answer is that auras are both fixed and changeable. This answer can only make sense when you take the nature of auras into consideration. Simple auras, such as those of plants or less intelligent animals, will remain at a constant. This is due to the fact that such auras lack the mental and emotional dimensions found in auras of humans and intelligent animals. The more complex a being's mind is, the more complex its aura will be. In contrast, the simpler the mind is, the simpler the aura will be. Thus, basic life forms will have constant auras. Alternatively, more complex beings will have auras that are changeable, and these changes will reflect such things as mood, physical and mental wellbeing and a whole host of other factors.

The aura as a reflection of who we are

One tradition holds that even people have a constant element within their aura. This can be explained by the layers of an aura. While outer layers may be more likely to change due to environmental factors, emotional states and other elements that are in flux the inner layer is more constant as it is a reflection of the individual's true self. If you take away the aura component and ask the question "are people changeable or permanent?" the truth becomes easier to understand. Just as the base nature of a person remains fairly fixed, while the day to day reality of the person is subject to change, the condition of the aura is the same. The base layer of an aura reflects the true nature of a person. Therefore, if a person is insightful, highly energetic and without inner conflict, their base layer will appear bright, vibrant and serene on a regular basis. Only if they were to go through some experience that changed who they are would this layer change in appearance.

Needless to say, people can develop and evolve over the course of their life. However, it should be realized that few people truly change on a fundamental level. Even the greatest transformation will rarely change a person much in terms of their true nature. Any change or development can usually be seen in terms of details, not the essence of who the person is. This constancy of being is what keeps the aura's base layer constant in appearance. The adage "a tiger can't change its stripes" holds just as true for auras as it does for the nature of a person.

The aura as a source of information

The outer layers of a person's aura can change, however, and this is due to the fact that those layers serve a completely different purpose. Unlike the base layer that can be seen as the virtual soul of a person, the outer layers are more like the emotions and condition of the person at any given time. Here is where change is not only possible, but it is expected. No person is capable of being in the same mood twenty-four hours a day, seven days a week. Instead, their mood will change based on what they are doing, how they are feeling and who they are with. These changes will cause the outer layers of their aura to change as well. Everything from color to brightness and even vibration will be influenced by the moment to moment emotions of the individual. Thus, if a person is angry, you can expect the outer layers of their aura to become red in color, possibly brighter in intensity and usually more agitated in vibration. However, as the person calms down the color will return to a calmer color, the brightness may reduce, and the vibration will become more serene.

Another way that outer layers of an aura can change is through changes in a person's health and wellbeing. When a person is healthy, their aura will be more vibrant, and the colors will be richer. Alternatively, when a person becomes sick, fatigued or emotionally distraught, their aura will take on a different appearance. Outer layers of an aura can become muted due to sickness and fatigue, and colors can become washed out in nature. Dull auras reflect low levels of energy, and yellow or brown colors are usually a sign of physical or mental illness. In a way, the outer colors of an aura act much like air. When air is healthy, it is clear, brisk and fresh. However, when the air is filled with pollution, toxins or other dangerous elements, it appears clouded, discolored and unpleasant in appearance. This is how you know whether or not air is safe to breathe. Similarly, the outer layers of a person's aura tell you whether or not they are healthy and safe to be around.

Fortunately, the outer layers of the aura will improve when the health and wellbeing of the individual is restored. In the case of physical illness, the aura will improve when the person receives medical treatment, or changes their diet and exercise regimen. However, in the case of mental illness, the aura will only improve when the individual receives psychological treatment or they change the habits in their daily life that lead to mental distress. In this way, the appearance of the outer layers of an aura should not be seen as fixed, but instead, they should be seen as indicators. A healthy aura shows that a person is living right and in good overall health. In this case, no changes need to be made. An unhealthy aura suggests that a person isn't living right, resulting in health issues that need to be addressed. Such indications should be seen as a call for change in habits, the need to seek treatment, or a combination of the two. Only by taking action can the necessary changes be made to restore the person to their natural state of health and wellbeing.

Chapter 14: How to Cleanse Your Aura

While the base aura of a person is relatively constant, the outer layers are usually in a state of flux. This means that they can change depending on a person's state of mind, physical health, and wellbeing or any other aspect that might influence how a person feels at any given time. A common question that arises is what to do if you recognize negative issues in your own aura. Some issues are relatively straightforward and simple to solve, such as getting some sleep should your aura indicate that you are fatigued. However, other issues may require some extra effort on your part in order to affect positive change. The technique for "fixing" your aura is commonly referred to as "cleansing". This chapter will reveal several techniques for cleansing your aura, thereby restoring your health and wellbeing from within.

Using nature to cleanse your aura

One of the most effective ways to cleanse your aura is to

leave the hustle and bustle of everyday life and retreat into nature. A good long walk in the woods can go a long way to restoring peace of mind and increasing your energy levels. Everyone knows that trees and green plants breathe in harmful gasses such as carbon dioxide and release oxygen in return. Just as they cleanse the air you breathe they can also cleanse your energies. By spending half an hour in nature on a daily basis, you can reduce anxiety, stress, and general negativity, all things that serve to diminish the appearance of your aura. The end result is that your aura will be revitalized, restoring its natural brightness and clarity once again.

Another way in which nature can cleanse your aura is through the use of herbs and essential oils. Whether you choose to burn essential oils during meditation or you choose to put them into a hot bath is up to you. The bottom line is that by breathing in natural fragrances such as lavender, eucalyptus or sage, you will begin to release toxic energies from your body and mind, thereby restoring your aura to full health and vitality. For best results, you should use such oils or herbs in a relaxed environment, such as meditation or a bath. Additionally, results are increased the longer you expose yourself to the herbs. If you can spare half an hour a day, you will be able to achieve immediate and significant results.

Increasing your energy levels

In many ways, the health and wellbeing of your aura is no different than the health and wellbeing of your body. This makes sense since, as discussed previously, your aura represents your physical condition among other things. That said, it should be no surprise that some of the things that serve to improve your physical health will also serve to improve the health and vitality of your aura. An example of this is exercise. If your aura appears dull and tired, the chances are your energy levels are low. One of the best ways to fix this is to increase your energy levels through regular exercise. Even a brisk 10 minute walk each and every day can make a big difference in terms of your energy.

Another way that energy can be affected is by the food you eat. When you eat junk food, such as fried foods, chips, ice cream and the like you fill your body with heavy calories and sugars, things that actually decrease your energy levels. However, when you eat healthier foods such as vegetables, foods rich in protein and the like you will increase your energy levels. Therefore, any habits that are proven to improve your physical health and wellbeing will also serve to improve the health and wellbeing of your aura.

Surrounding yourself with positivity

 In addition to being affected by the things you take in, your energy levels can also be affected by your surroundings. This is particularly true with regard to the people you surround yourself with. It is common knowledge that when a person spends a lot of time with negative people, they will inevitably become negative in their own thoughts, words and actions. You never hear of a successful person having negative friends. Instead, the most successful people tend to spend their time with people who provide inspiration, support, and much-needed motivation. Therefore, if your aura is dim and weak, it could be a result of the energy you are surrounded by. The best way to fix this is to spend more time with people who are highly energetic, full of positivity and who offer constant support and affection.

Another common source of negativity can be the information you take in on a daily basis. It's no secret that news shows, social media and other such sources of information tend to focus on highly negative content. When you expose yourself to this negativity for long, your energy will begin to change for the worse. The impact that information has on your energy is the same as the impact that food has on your body. Just as junk food will cause fatigue and ill health, so too, negative information will cause depression and anxiety. These conditions will create a dull and dirty aura, one that reflects the negative nature of your energies. The only solution to this problem is to change your information diet. Rather than subjecting yourself to negativity day after day begin exposing yourself to positive information. This can take any form, including playing games, engaging in hobbies or any other form of mental activity that creates a positive impact on your energy. Once you reduce the amount of negative information feeding your mind your aura will begin to be restored to its full health once again.

Restoring peace of mind

Sometimes the problem is less about the information you are receiving and more about the information that is already in your mind. Anyone who has dark thoughts floating through their head at any given time will have a dark aura to match. These thoughts don't have to be anything too sinister in nature; rather they just have to be generally negative. Any time you see yourself as inadequate or not good enough you create negative energy. This energy will reveal itself in your aura. Likewise, such emotions as greed, envy, anger, and hatred will also create large amounts of negative energy. It's no wonder that religious figures such as Buddha, Jesus, and the Dali Lama encourage their followers to abandon such emotions and fill their hearts and minds with love, compassion, and other such positive emotions.

In order to restore your aura to full health, you need to restore your peace of mind. The first step is to take the time to recognize all of the negative thoughts that you entertain each and every day. If you constantly see yourself as inferior, you need to begin to build your self-confidence. Replace thoughts of inadequacy with thoughts of confidence and high self-worth. Additionally, remove any anger and hostility you have toward others and replace it with thoughts and feelings of a more positive nature. This doesn't mean that you have to start loving your enemies, although that would be what the religious icons would recommend. Rather, all you have to do is focus your mind and heart on the people and things you love. Don't let bad things and bad people control your heart and mind. Instead, allow the people and things you love to fill your mind with happy thoughts and your heart with the bliss that it deserves. Once you do this, your aura will become bright and vibrant again.

Conclusion

Now that you have read this book, you have all the information you need in order to develop your ability to see and read auras. Whether you are a religious person or not, you now understand that auras don't require you to follow any particular tradition or belief system. Furthermore, you can be sure that reading auras is not against any religious rule or law that might create problems in your life. Instead, the ability to see and read auras is something that is natural, safe and beneficial, both to the reader and the person whose aura is being read. The only thing left to do is to begin practicing the process so that you can open your mind to the wonderful world of reading auras. Remember, start slow and simply allow the process to take place. The very best of luck to you!

If you enjoyed the book, please consider leaving us a positive review on Amazon

Recommended Reading and Audio Books

Auras, Clairvoyance & Psychic Development: Energy Fields and Reading People
https://amzn.to/2SxjJr9

Third Eye: Third Eye, Mind Power, Intuition & Psychic Awareness: Spiritual Enlightenment
https://amzn.to/2qre9tX

MIND CONTROL: Manipulation, Deception and Persuasion Exposed: Human Psychology
https://amzn.to/2Jrse2X

Red Light Therapy: Guide to Natural Healing Light Medicine
https://amzn.to/2Q6ISYl

Sources

http://stylecaster.com/auras-guide/

https://www.sciencedaily.com/releases/2012/05/120504110024.htm

https://www.mindbodygreen.com/0-25407/what-is-an-aura-and-how-can-you-see-yours.html

https://atlantisrisingmagazine.com/article/the-human-aura-real-or-imaginary/

https://www.speakingtree.in/allslides/the-scientific-evidence-of-human-aura/119278

http://www.biofieldglobal.org/what-is-human-aura.html

https://www.theepochtimes.com/what-are-the-auras-around-people-seen-in-photos_668239.html

https://www.thiaoouba.com/seeau.htm

https://www.buildingbeautifulsouls.com/symbols-meanings/aura-colors-meanings/auras-real/

https://www.buildingbeautifulsouls.com/symbols-meanings/aura-colors-meanings/how-to-see-auras/

https://www.buildingbeautifulsouls.com/symbols-meanings/aura-colors-meanings/

http://uk.iacworld.org/how-to-see-auras-for-beginners/

https://www.learning-mind.com/5-questions-about-auras-answered-by-a-person-who-is-able-to-see-energy/

http://www.lunalunamagazine.com/dark/cleanse-your-aura

https://www.gaia.com/lp/content/cleanse-your-aura-for-spring/

https://www.quora.com/Does-our-aura-change-as-we-grow

https://www.gotquestions.org/auras-Christian.html

https://www.openbible.info/topics/auras

http://www.chinabuddhismencyclopedia.com/en/index.php?title=Aura

https://www.paganspath.com/meta/aura.htm

https://vidyutbodha.wordpress.com/gautama-buddha-prabashvara/

https://en.wikipedia.org/wiki/Prabashvara

http://www.spiritofra.com/psychophysics%204.htm

https://www.consciouslifestylemag.com/aura-reading-cleansing-energy-field/

http://www.chimachine4u.com/chi.html

https://gostica.com/aura-science/layers-of-the-aura/2/

Made in the USA
San Bernardino, CA
24 January 2019